And we all live on a tiny speck in space called Planet Earth.

A WONDERFUL WORLD

What do we need to live on our home in space?
Air to breathe, water to drink, food to eat and
somewhere to shelter from the weather.
The Earth gives us all these things.

THE BLUE PLANET

Water covers 70% of Planet Earth – it could be called Planet Water really! And even we humans are made up of about 60% water.

Our oceans and seas are full of treasures – precious corals and fish, seahorses, whales and dolphins.

Salt comes from the sea.

Bet you didn't know that sea plants make MOST of our oxygen!

Can you find ME every time you turn a page?

The Great Big Green Book

Mary Hoffman and Ros Asquith

OUR HOME IN SPACE

The universe is a huge place, bigger than any of us can imagine.

But we can't drink salty sea water. For that we need rivers, lakes and streams and the rain that pours into them from the sky. Our rivers are full of fish we can eat.

We should try to keep all our water clean so that the fish and plants in it stay alive. We also need enough to drink and to water the crops we grow.

THE GREEN PLANET

Plants and trees are amazing.
We get so much from them – shelter,
food, clothes, even kinds of medicine.
Especially from the tropical rainforests,
where evergreen trees drink up the
heavy rainfall all year round.
But large parts of the rainforests
are cut down every year
to make way for farmland.

EVERY BREATH WE TAKE

Plants even breathe in the stuff we breathe out and keep the air clean. But we are making them work extra hard if we put lots of dirty smoke into the air.

We look after insects and animals

AND WE CLEAN the AIR

Help us!

So many cars and lorries and factories are pouring out fumes that the trees might not be able to keep up with cleaning the air.

We should try to find ways of keeping
air clean enough for us and animals
to breathe.

CLIMATE CHANGE

No fish in the desert. No mice in the floods.

Our planet is getting warmer, most scientists agree, because of all the stuff we burn. This extra heat changes our weather. Some parts of the world have more storms, floods or hurricanes, while others get less and less rainfall.

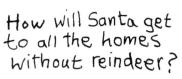

How will Santa get to all the homes without reindeer?

The natural homes of animals – their habitats – change because of the changes in the weather. Some animals have to learn to adapt.

Mum! Our home is shrinking!

Some penguins are laying eggs earlier so there are more of them.

But others might die out...

ALL CREATURES GREAT AND SMALL

All animals – including humans – are
part of a very delicate balance in nature.

Elephants, tigers, gorillas, blue whales, polar bears, red pandas and rhinos are all in danger, as well as many other animals.

We help plants to grow.

A WALE

Elefant
ELEPHANT

Red PANDa

Rhino

IN DANGER

Bees like trees.

Nearly ONE THIRD of our food depends on BEES!

HONEY

We help the Earth turn.

We have to protect our animals because we all share this world and all have a part to play in it.

A RACE AGAINST TIME

Animals aren't the only creatures in danger.
If we lose too many trees and too much of our
natural water becomes dirty or dries up, humans
could end up extinct – like the dinosaurs!

The ways we keep our homes warm – or cool – and brightly lit won't last forever. We need to think of new ideas to give us the heat and light we need.

Running keeps you warm.

So does cycling.

TURN OFF LIGHTS

SHUT DOORS

THICK curtains

Use LED bulbs

UNPLUG EVERYTHING

SAVE WATER, SAVE ENERGY

We should all try to save water, gas and electricity in our homes. Sometimes lots of small things can add up to BIG savings.

Can you use a lower setting on the washing machine? Dry clothes outside if you possibly can.

It's hard because usually the grown-ups make these decisions – but you can talk to them about it.

ROUND AND ROUND

Instead of wasting things we don't want
any more by throwing them away,
we could give them to someone
else who wants them.
This is called 'recycling'.

We are also doing recycling
if we buy clothes and other
things from charity shops.

And think of all the plastic,
cardboard and paper that fills
up our houses every day.
It can all be recycled and
used again.

Instead of piling up smelly rubbish
or burying it in the ground, we can use
lots of it to make compost –
which turns into new earth.

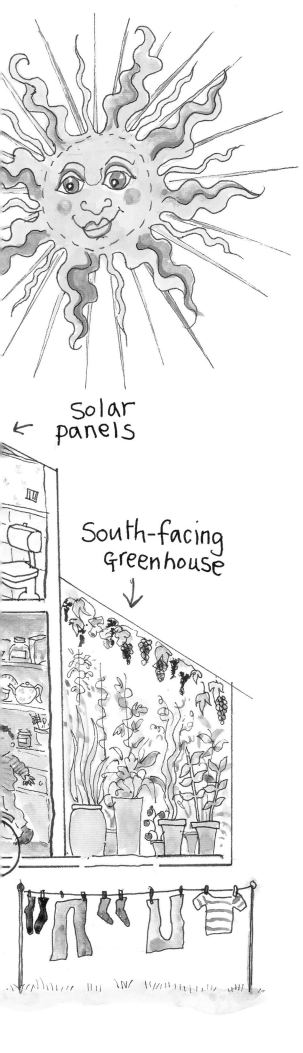

Scientists are working on ways to make nuclear energy safer.

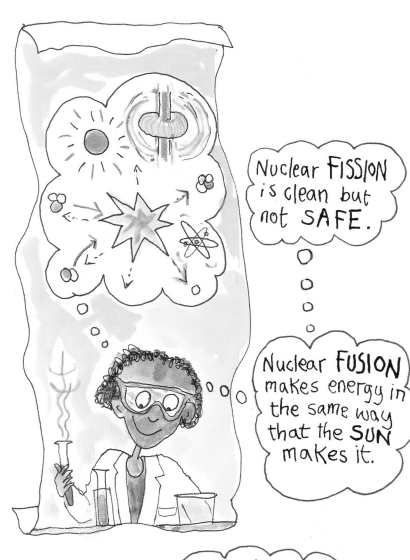

MAKE IT NEW

We have got used to living in a throwaway world but all sorts of things can be mended – bicycles, clothes, toys, furniture.

Looks NEW now.

I made Mum a shirt out of old underpants.

Whoops!

I love my OLD teddy best.

We just need to learn the skills of mending again and stop thinking everything has to be brand new and in the latest fashion.

GO SLOW

We need to slow down a bit. Every time someone whizzes across the world in a fast plane there is more pollution in the air.

Planes also bring food thousands of miles away from where it has grown, so that we can eat strawberries and other things all year round.

We could take time to grow our own food near our homes in allotments – even window boxes! Or if we can't do that we could buy food in the season it grows in our own countries.

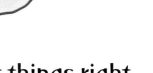

ASK QUESTIONS

Grown-ups don't always get things right,
so don't be afraid to ask questions.

How do you make electricity?

How could you feed everyone in the world?

Should we walk to school?

Why don't we take the bus instead of the car?

How does water get INTO a tap?

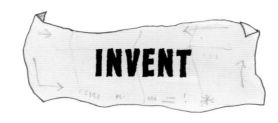

The Earth's problems won't just go away without our help. Some of the best ideas to help the planet are coming from really young people, like the 18-year-old Dutch boy, Boyan Slat, who invented a way to clear the oceans of plastic. Or the 16-year-old girl from Egypt, Azza Abdel Hamid Faiad, who has discovered a process to turn waste plastic into fuel.

But if most of the planet is desert it'll be easy to bury our heads in the sand.

DRINK ONLY TAP WATER

Or puddles?

Solar-powered flying trainers

$y=mc^2$!

Maybe you can think of ideas and devices to help save the planet in all the ways it most needs?

IF it CRASHES it WILL BOUNCE!

SAFe ruBBer WiND-Powered CAR THAt RUNS on Water

BUT a WOLF COULD blow it down

CARdBoArd house

FLOATING $CITIES for when SEA riSes

2,000 yrs OLD

EverlaSTing CLoTHES

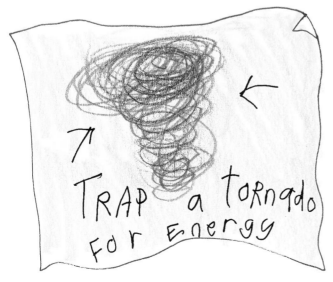

TRAP a TorNado For EnergY

SHoeS WITH Springs

BACK TO BLUE

Can you imagine our planet as beautiful as it used to be? You could be the ones to make it beautiful again, with the things you do and the ideas you have.

Your planet needs
YOU

Yes, YOU – the ones reading this book!

SOME USEFUL WORDS

Allotment – a plot of land someone can rent to grow fruit and vegetables on.

Climate Change/Global Warming – a change in local or global weather caused by humans burning fossil fuels.

Conservation – not wasting things and finding ways to look after life on our planet.

Energy – power to produce heat and light and make engines work.

Environment – the natural world around us in our neighbourhood or the whole planet.

Extinct – having no living members left.

Food miles – the distance food is brought from where it is grown to where it is sold in shops.

Fossil fuels – natural fuels like coal or gas, formed in the distant past by dead trees or other organisms.

Green – not just a colour! It means caring about our environment.

Habitat – place where an animal, plant or human lives.

Nuclear Power – energy produced when atoms are split (Nuclear Fission) or when atoms are joined (Nuclear Fusion).

Oxygen – the part of the air we breathe that all animals need to keep them alive.

Pollution – dirty, harmful or poisonous substances in the air or water.

Rainforest – a forest, usually a tropical one, where the rainfall each year adds up to 406 cms (160 inches).

Recycling – finding useful materials in things that others no longer want.

Solar Power – power from the rays of the sun.

MORE FACTS

Azza Abdel Hamid Faiad.
Look him up on www.smartplanet.com

Boyan Slat.
He has a TED talk on this subject on YouTube

SOME USEFUL WEBSITES

Car-sharing: *www.liftshare.com*

Climate Science: *www.realclimate.org*

Fairtrade: *www.fairtrade.org.uk*

Green Living: *www.greenlivingonline.com*

Looking after animals: National Geographic Kids *www.kids.nationalgeographic.co.uk*

Looking after trees: Forest Stewardship Council *www.fsc.org;* Rainforest Alliance *www.rainforest-alliance.org;* The Woodland Trust *www.naturedetectives.org.uk;* Planet Ark *www.planetark.com*

Meet the Greens: *www.meetthegreens.org; www.treehugger.com; www.thedailygreen.com*

Recycling: *www.recyclezone.org.uk; www.freecycle.org; www.recyclenow.com*

Saving water: *www.wateraid.org*

Worldwide Fund for Nature: *www.wwf.org*

For Freddie and George Sherry, my nephews,
who will inherit the Earth – MH

To Lola, Lenny, Lucille and Babette, with love – RA

JANETTA OTTER-BARRY BOOKS

Text copyright © Mary Hoffman 2015
Illustrations copyright © Ros Asquith 2015

First published in Great Britain and in the USA in 2015 by
Frances Lincoln Children's Books,
74-77 White Lion Street, London N1 9PF
www.franceslincoln.com

A CIP catalogue record for this book
is available from the British Library

ISBN 978-1-84780-445-7

Illustrated with watercolours

Set in Green

Printed in China
1 3 5 7 9 8 6 4 2